SERENDIPITY

How to Attract a Life You Love

SERENDIPITY

How to Attract a Life You Love

SECOND EDITION

Joshua Rosenthal, MScEd

FOUNDER AND DIRECTOR, INSTITUTE FOR INTEGRATIVE NUTRITION

www.integrativenutrition.com

Serendipity: How to Attract a Life You Love

ISBN: 978-1-941908-05-1 (paperback)
ISBN: 978-1-941908-04-4 (e-book)

Copyright © 2018 by Integrative Nutrition, Inc.

Library of Congress Control Number: 2017962220

Published by Integrative Nutrition, Inc., New York, NY
www.integrativenutrition.com

Notice: This book is not intended to replace recommendations or advice from physicians or other healthcare providers. Rather, it is intended to help you make informed decisions about your health and to cooperate with your healthcare provider in a joint quest for optimal wellness. If you suspect you have a medical problem, we urge you to seek medical attention from a competent healthcare provider.

Printed in USA

10 9 8 7 6 5 4 3 2 1

Second Edition

Special thanks to Michaela Rowland, Lula Brown, Shannon Lagasse, Joline Seavey, and Tim Tate for their support and dedication to the success of this project.

OTHER TITLES BY JOSHUA ROSENTHAL

CONTENTS

FOREWORD

S erendipity is a magical experience that is an unfolding of our deepest desire. Such experiences can range from simple things like receiving a call from someone you had been thinking about, to something as profound as meeting someone who completely transforms your life.

When I first met Joshua almost 10 years ago, it was a moment of serendipity that brought us together and changed my life in unimaginable ways. I was a student at the Institute for Integrative Nutrition, the school Joshua founded. Like many of the students who enroll at IIN, I was in pursuit of a more meaningful life and career. During class, I told a student next to me that I wanted to speak with Joshua about work as a lawyer for the school, because the legal work I was doing just didn't feel like my calling. Since Joshua was in the middle of teaching, and I am a shy person, the chances that I would get this message through to him personally were pretty close to zero. At the break, my classmate encouraged me, "Go speak with him now!" And I found myself, rather uncharacteristically, jumping out of my seat and making my way to the front of the class where Joshua was standing. When I reached him, I introduced myself, brought my hands together in front of my heart, and explained that I wanted to do something that was more in alignment with my soul's purpose.

In that moment, time seemed to stand still for the both of us, as we sensed something deeper was transpiring. My vision of contributing to IIN's legal team did not manifest, however. It was clear I was being led into a life more deeply aligned with who I am, which includes being Joshua's life partner.

Serendipity has a way of delivering to us our soul's purpose. Very often, though, this happens in a way that we don't expect. The more we are present and in the flow of life, the more we experience and notice these moments and the more we're able to use them to enhance our lives.

Having been around Joshua for many years and having learned the same process from him that he outlines in this book, I now experience more frequent and magical serendipitous events. It has changed the course of my life in profound ways that continually bring me closer to who I am and my purpose.

Interestingly, as I sat down to write this foreword, I realized I had already written a foreword years ago for a journal that I created to track all of the amazing serendipitous moments that we continually witnessed happening to Joshua. I always joke with him that his head is like a powerful antenna. Joshua has a deep level of awareness and presence. He knows there is no real separation between you and me and the world around us. It's not just a theory; Joshua lives it day to day and moment to moment, which is evidenced by the way he effortlessly glides through life.

He seems to pick these meaningful moments out of the ether wherever we go, which is always wildly fascinating to us both. Most of us overlook these sometimes subtle events, brush them off as coincidence, or notice synchronicities but then don't follow through with where they are leading us. By contrast, Joshua immediately recognizes and follows through on them, which inevitably leads to something greater that supports the development of his life path in some way.

Perhaps it is a result of his deeply inquisitive and analytical nature, his dedication to unearthing the most profound truths, or his many travels to India, where he learned to live in a space beyond the illusion of separation. Whatever the case, Joshua uses serendipitous events to guide the flow of his life and his mission, which, over time, has transformed thousands of peoples' lives and has begun to powerfully shift the healthcare paradigm by making health coaching more mainstream and available in 155 countries across the globe. It has led him to a life he never could have even imagined for himself.

Understanding the powerful nature of serendipity has changed my life. It has given me meaning, purpose, confidence, and connected me with my life partner. In this book, Joshua explains how you, too, can increase your experience of serendipity and use this magical, mystical process to enhance the success and fulfillment you have in all areas of your life.

ALEXANDRA ANZALONE

"Joshua uses serendipitous events to guide the flow of his life and his mission, which, over time, has transformed thousands of peoples' lives and has begun to powerfully shift the healthcare paradigm by making health coaching more mainstream and available in 155 countries across the globe. It has led him to a life he never could have even imagined for himself."

HOW TO USE THIS BOOK

Serendipity is a huge part of my life, and sharing it with you is part of my mission to change the lives of as many people as possible. Throughout this book, you'll see real-life examples of serendipity in action from people I know. These serve as social proof—if they can do it, you can do it, too.

You'll also see exercises throughout the book. Keep a journal handy so you can complete them in real time as you read. I don't necessarily have all of the answers, but I want to ask you the questions that will help you find the answers.

I can't wait to start this journey with you!

INTRODUCTION

Take a moment to stop and imagine what your world might look like if you had the power to attract endless positivity. I'll bet your mind paints a pretty amazing picture.

Since beginning the journey that the Institute of Integrative Nutrition (IIN) was born of, I've had the good fortune to meet, counsel, and teach tens of thousands of people. As a result, my awareness of how the human body and psyche functions has grown exponentially and evolved into a profound understanding that I would never have gained if not for the experiences I've had along the way.

Over that time, I've become highly sensitive to the millions of connections in life and how they can nurture a being—physically, emotionally, and spiritually—to bring about accomplishments and advancements that one may have only dreamed of before. When all of those connections gel, and a person finds that they are in the flow of life, the powers of synchronicity and serendipity suddenly become apparent and abundant.

Not sure you know what I'm talking about? In all likelihood, you've experienced synchronicity, serendipity, or both at some point in your life, even if you didn't realize it at the time. It can be something as simple as when you're thinking about a song, and it comes on the radio or noticing the clock at that rare moment when it reads 11:11. It can also be something much more grandiose, like meeting someone in a coffee shop who just happens to be hiring for a position you're interested in. I'll go into more depth about the difference between synchronicity and serendipity a little later, but for now I'll put it as simply as possible: When any seemingly random, yet coincidental, event occurs, that is synchronicity. When you add a distinctly positive effect or outcome to that event, it evolves into serendipity.

When we start acknowledging the small stuff and celebrating it, the big stuff is more likely to come. A few years ago, I was hardly spending any time in New York City. Yet, when I was there for only one weekend in the spring, I ran into a dear friend of mine from Miami while walking down 5th Avenue. Although he was only in town for a few hours, it gave us the time to reconnect that we would not have otherwise had. Granted, that occurrence wasn't necessarily a life-changing experience, but I've come to realize that becoming aware of the serendipitous events that are already taking place, I invite more of them into my daily life.

Most people brush off synchronicity and serendipity as mere coincidences. But the truth is that the people who experience frequent instances of serendipity are always attracting the things they need into their lives because they operate on a different wavelength. They're the people you might look at and think, "Wow. Such amazing things always happen to her. She's so lucky."

However, luck isn't necessarily the driving force behind it all. In fact, a lot of scientific research exists in the realms of positivity and positive attractive forces, and it's been proven that, on a molecular level, our thoughts and actions actually create our reality. Pretty cool, right?

I have spent a lot of time thinking about this subject and researching what's different about the people who experience consistent synchronicity and serendipity in their lives. We've all had the experience at some point of being in the right place at the right time or wanting to talk to someone, and they call at just that moment. Yet there are still so many people out there who are feeling stuck in their lives, whether in relationships, careers, or even their own bodies, which means that they haven't been able to tap into the true power of these awesome forces that are so instrumental in helping us to achieve our dream lives.

Those who are having big, serendipitous events occur in their lives – like getting called to go on a television show when they've had it on their vision board for years – are engaging in certain behaviors that allow serendipity to flow to them more freely. I've had so many of these experiences myself, and they happen when I feel healthy, supported, loved, and aligned with my mission.

Serendipity has been such a powerful and vital tool in both the building of my business and the happiness I have in my everyday life that I feel compelled to share everything that I've learned and experienced with you. I believe that everyone has a right to the joy that comes with finding yourself in the flow of life.

What you're receiving from the universe is in tune with what you're sending out into it, and I can hardly wait to help you get started on creating a roadmap to your own positive existence and getting everything you want in your life.

Are you ready to get started?

1 THE POWER OF SERENDIPITY

"Some of the greatest things, as I understand, they have come about by serendipity, the greatest discoveries."

—ALAN ALDA

Serendipity is a truly powerful tool you can use to attract almost anything into your life. When it's working for you, the world is your oyster. Without knowing how to use it, life can seem to take place by happenstance. Before we dive deeper, let's begin first with grasping the concept of serendipity and differentiating it from synchronicity.

So what exactly are synchronicity and serendipity?

By definition, synchronicity is "the simultaneous occurrence of events that appear significantly related but have no discernible causal connection."

An example of synchronicity is running into someone you know in an unlikely place, without any kind of obvious, specific, or positive outcome. You both just happen to be in the same place at the same time, unplanned. Usually an occurrence such as this is enough to make a person stop and take notice, due to its improbable nature, while another who is not quite as present may miss the significance.

Now serendipity, on the other hand, is defined as "the faculty or phenomenon of finding valuable or pleasant things not sought for"—or, taking a synchronistic event and adding a decidedly beneficial outcome to it.

All serendipitous events are synchronistic, but not all synchronistic events are serendipitous. Serendipity is an explicitly positive experience, whereas synchronicity could be a mundane or extraordinary "coincidence."

So let's take that previous example of synchronicity and add a specifically positive outcome to the scenario, such as the person you ran into having a connection with the company for which you've applied for a job. Do you see the difference?

THE ROOTS OF SYNCHRONICITY

Carl Jung, the famous Swiss psychiatrist who was an early protégé and avid supporter of Sigmund Freud, is one of my favorite people, and he served as a great inspiration for me to start investigating synchronicity and serendipity further. He coined the term "synchronicity" in the early 20th century, explaining it as two or more events that are a little too perfect to seem real, also known as a meaningful coincidence or the acausal connecting principle.

For Jung, the acausal connecting principle and synchronicity were reveals for the unification between mind and matter. He believed that so-called "coincidences" are actually events whose sole purpose is to exhibit, through meaning, the link between mental and physical occurrences. Jung made so many big contributions to the world of psychology, but this was perhaps his most fascinating: the inception and development of the idea that there's more to life than our physical senses can perceive.

Of course, as I mentioned previously, we don't always take notice of synchronistic events, nor do we have an understanding of their causes. However, just because we're not paying close attention doesn't mean that there isn't a cause, and as an individual becomes more balanced, present, and in tune with their environment they will be more likely to recognize the universe's fastball when it's delivered and the unfolding pattern that it represents.

Physical manifestations of the principles of focus and attention may be much easier for some to relate to. Perhaps you notice that when you exercise or move your body in particular ways, it helps to get your day flowing properly. Or for those of you who meditate, you may find that using meditation to center your mind on a daily basis seems to increase the amount of positive energy in your life. And for still others, getting connected can be as simple as taking a daily walk in nature. All of these are examples of ways in which people can find their own flow and, as a result, find themselves in the right place at the right time.

Synchronicity is the starting point for serendipity, and serendipity is where the magic truly begins.

WHY WE WANT SERENDIPITY & REVERSE SERENDIPITY

Perhaps you're starting to wonder what all the fuss is about. Simply stated, serendipity makes things a whole lot easier. When it's happening, you feel like your life is flowing. Your shoulders release and drop, and you feel like you can breathe. When you're in the flow, your life is in alignment, and you're full of joy and natural energy.

Have you ever seen a hawk in flight? He soars effortlessly above the trees, riding the wind currents with ease. He is not flapping his wings incessantly, trying to rise higher like some of the other birds do. He's found the flow of the wind and flies effortlessly. That's serendipity.

We can live in much the same way. The people you encounter who always seem to have incredible luck, who always seem to be full of energy and vitality – those are the hawks, the people who have found the flow of their life and are in it, free from the need to exert so much energy to obtain the things they value. That's because the truth is that synchronicity and serendipity are naturally occurring phenomena, gifts that we all enter this world in possession of. So when they're not happening for an individual, it signals that something is off.

Do you know someone who always seems to have bad luck or who can never quite catch a break? Do you find that events infrequently turn in your favor? Or perhaps, simply, the world around you seems flat and dull where it was once vibrant and alive? These are all telltale signs of what is called reverse serendipity, which is a term that was coined to describe being in a state of misalignment with the universe.

When you're healthy, happy, and living in harmony, serendipity naturally flows in your life. However, the opposite is also true. When you're feeding your body poorly, doing work you hate, participating in a toxic relationship, or not working your body enough through physical exercise, things will never go as smoothly as they could.

When you're living out of alignment, you're more likely to feel irritated, tired, and scared. You wake up anxious and are hesitant to face the day, feeling like the whole world is against you and everyone is plotting to take you down. When you're not living in harmony, you're likely to have a hard time connecting with and trusting people, and you may feel like nothing ever seems to go your way.

Do some or all of these descriptions sound familiar to you? Do you experience these things in your daily life?

HOW WE LOSE SERENDIPITY & HOW WE GET IT BACK

Do you feel like you're always rushing? So many people in this modern world feel like they're always behind, never have enough time, and are never good enough.

Busy-ness is a common affliction of today's fast-paced society. Over-booked calendars, fast food, too much stress, and too little sleep are all symptoms of a civilization that has gained technology and "stuff" but has slowly watched its humanity slip away, gazing endlessly into our smart-phones instead of connecting with the people we care about and letting the everyday wonders of life pass us by unnoticed. We've become enslaved by technological advancements that were only meant to serve us.

The rampant busy-ness that so many experience on a regular basis speaks to an underlying issue of imbalance. In traditional Chinese medi-cine (TCM), balance is represented by the yin and the yang. For example, in terms of food, yin food is sweet, such as fruit or sugar, whereas yang foods are savory—seaweed, for example.

TCM also applies the concepts of yin and yang to energy and life force. Yin energy represents the feminine and is expansive, loving, restful, and flowing. So if you spend a day relaxing around your home or enjoy some restoration at the spa, that brings yin energy into your life. Yang energy, on the other hand, is focused and serious, the masculine side. The days spent aggressively developing your business plan or productively com-pleting a long list of tasks, that's yang energy.

These energies don't necessarily have anything to do with whether you're female or male. They're just metaphors for expansive and contractive energy, respectively. Both men and women require both types of energy to thrive and feel balanced. If you spend too much time in a relaxed state, you become too yin and feel purposeless and lost. To the contrary, if you spend too much time working or studying, you'll begin to feel stressed by the lack of pleasure and play in your life. It is only when these energies are balanced that one can feel completely at ease and in tune. That balance is also a prerequisite for serendipity.

Let's take this beyond the topic of balance and discuss an even more vital topic—the fact that many of us have lost touch with our instincts, choosing to trust societal messages delivered through mass media over our own inner voices. Instructions on who you are and what you need are delivered both consciously and subconsciously via television, the Internet, social media outlets, and advertisements, which, when consistently reinforced, insidiously transition from suggestion to almighty truth. Furthermore, our loved ones reinforce these imported beliefs, regurgitating the same information to create a continual feedback loop.

This disconnection from our instincts has led us to stop using our hearts as our guides, choosing instead to trust in our egotistical and ever-rationalizing minds. Granted, the human mind can be an incredible tool. However, what was once meant to be used exclusively as our tool has instead become our driving force and all too often runs rampant, drunk with power.

The only way to return to serendipity is to place our trust in our hearts and instincts in the present moment. When we're able to do this, we often find that what the universe has in store for us is grander than anything we could have ever have imagined.

You see, serendipity is an attractive force in and of itself: The more you pay attention to and take notice of synchronistic and serendipitous events, the more they will flow toward you. Keep the saying in mind, "What you focus on grows, and what you appreciate appreciates."

I would like to urge you to begin your quest for more serendipity by getting a journal and starting to keep track of the synchronistic events already happening in your life.

Write down what's happening in your life before and after synchronistic and serendipitous events. Take note of any behaviors or actions that help you attract more of what you want and create the life of your dreams.

Try asking yourself these questions:

What are a few synchronistic and/or serendipitous things that have happened to you in the past year?

What helps you to be more present to synchronicity and serendipity?

What's going on in your physical, mental, and emotional bodies before and after these events?

What blocks to synchronicity and serendipity have you noticed in your life?

In addition, start examining the five primary areas of your life for dysfunction and/or neglect: food, relationships, career, exercise, and spirituality. Take a few moments to write this down, and honestly rate each on a scale of 1–10 so that you have a starting point to reference.

Next, we're going to take that starting point and use it to discover how to follow the roadmap that will lead you back to a life filled with love, joy, and a lot of serendipity.

2 FOLLOW THE ROADMAP

"Maintaining an open mind is essential when exploring the unknown, but allowing one's brains to fall out in the process is inadvisable."

—DEAN RADIN

Once we begin to trust in the process of life, we develop a natural orbit of serendipity, very much like the orbit of the Earth around the sun. In order to do that, a high level of intimacy with one's internal workings is required.

You started this book by taking a moment to imagine what your life would look like if you were in the flow and your life were full of serendipity and positive forces. What did you see in that visualization? I'd like for you to take a moment and write down in your journal a description of what that life looks like to you, so you can reference it later.

Now let's talk about how you can get there.

As I touched on in chapter 1, true serendipity lives in your heart and gut. That means remaining centered in and connected to our hearts and bellies, rather than becoming wrapped up in our minds. It also means letting go of the ego—the judgmental voice in our heads—and trusting that everything will unfold the way it should.

Growing up, I was always asking myself, "What's really true? What's actually happening here?" Something always felt off for me—I felt different from everyone else. I knew that what I was hearing and seeing were not all there was to life. I saw this crack in the cosmic egg—a way in to a more serendipitous, deeper way of living. For me, it happened early in my life and made me view everything differently.

As a result, I find in the present that I have the power to slow things down and that my openness and stillness allow me to be a conduit for great things. I'm an open vessel. My life partner says that my head is like an antenna: I get signals that things are about to happen, and I use that skill to lead me forward.

Speaking of my partner, our first meeting is a prime example of going with your gut instinct. She demonstrated her trust in the universe the first time our paths crossed when she sprang out of her seat to talk to me, even though she's not usually a very forward person. She wanted to do pro bono legal work for the school and didn't even realize right away that I was already sensing a much deeper connection with her.

Time was standing still for me in that moment, and I realized something bigger was happening than just a new legal advisor coming into the picture. As it turns out, there were many synchronicities between us, and we would end up being together for a very long time.

When you listen to your instincts, you are welcoming serendipity into your life, so I don't recommend going against them by overanalyzing things before taking action. Too many people find opportunities slipping through their grasp because of hesitation and indecisiveness.

Think back on some past events of your own that did not turn out the way you would have liked for them to. What was it like when you were making the decisions connected to those events? Were you following your gut instinct or some other voice? Did you procrastinate on making those decisions instead of seizing the moment?

It's not difficult to detect when your life isn't in flow or when you're not getting the things you need from it. For example, if frustrating things keep happening at work, or you start getting physical symptoms from sitting still and looking at the computer all day, you need to take all of that into consideration when you're deciding whether your current job/career path is the right one for you.

Similarly, if your body keeps giving you hints to remove meat from your diet and go vegetarian, you should listen closely to those whispers. Not everything will make sense at first, but if you follow your heart and your gut, everything will fall into place.

Even when it's not obvious that all of these pieces are connected to your path, you can bet that they are. All of the little clues your body gives you—from both the physical and emotional realms—directly inform you about which steps you need to take next.

I find I'm able to hold an open space for serendipity to come in on a high level. For me, this happened somewhat naturally because I'm a highly sensitive person and a deep thinker who frequently focuses my attention inward. I'm also very independent and thrive with a lot of alone time. I've ensured that my living environment supports my inner life by choosing a home among the Berkshires where I'm able to spend a lot of time in nature.

Remember those antennae my partner accused me of having? Those are something you, too, can develop by checking in with yourself about how you honestly feel in different situations. Journaling, meditating, exercising, doing work you love, spending time with loved ones, and spending time by yourself are some of the best ways to accomplish this. These are the foundations for the concept of primary food.

We'll go deeper into primary food in chapter 3, but in short I can describe it as the idea that your life fuels you more than the food on your plate. Your relationships, career, exercise, and spirituality are the four main components of primary food. When your life is out of balance, no amount of healthy food—what I call secondary food—will make you feel better.

Ultimately, how our personal roadmap looks is very specific to our current needs. Its manifestation will depend on where we currently are in our lives, our surroundings, the situations we're dealing with, and what kind of answers we're seeking.

However, despite our individual differences, the keys to navigating any roadmap to serendipity remain the same:

- Remove the analytical mind from the process, and follow your gut instinct.
- Listen to the inner whispers of your body and heart.
- Cultivate a calm, centered, peaceful presence by maintaining a balance of primary food as well as yin and yang energies.

Are you excited to learn about primary food? Let's dive in!

Serendipitous Moments

Creating Your Roadmap

Georgia

In mid-2015, I was living in the suburbs of Chicago, and I was discovering just how badly misaligned I was with the life I wanted to be living. I had a job that was causing me extreme amounts of daily stress and physically draining me, and my romantic life was a complete disaster because I repeatedly chose unsuitable mate after unsuitable mate.

I finally decided one day that I'd had enough. I did some serious soul searching about what I really wanted out of my life and got clear with myself on exactly what my dreams were—what kind of profession I wanted, who my ideal long-term life mate would be, and the lifestyle I wanted to pursue. Within a year, I had found and settled down with my life partner, found my dream job, and started really living every day the fulfilling lifestyle I'd always wanted. Once I learned to ask the universe for what I needed and started working to get all of my primary foods in order, everything became amazing!

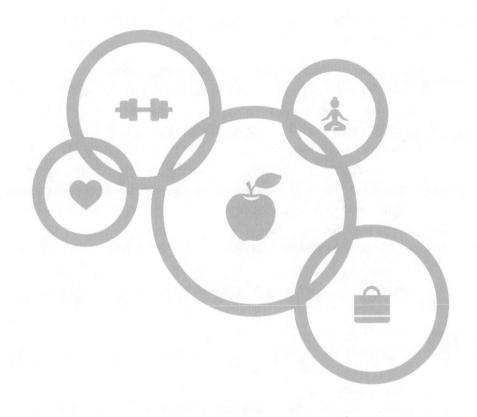

3 PRIMARY & SECONDARY FOODS

"Happiness is not a matter of intensity but of balance and order and rhythm and harmony."
                                                                  —THOMAS MERTON

When you're looking to bring more serendipity into your life, a primary factor is learning to maintain a long-term, overall balance. The first thought may go to diet when someone thinks of balance, that is "a balanced diet." However, I believe that there is much more to it than that.

It's obvious that there are many aspects of life that nourish us beyond food. Can you remember a time when you were freshly involved in a passionate relationship or had just taken on a new and exciting project? Life was stimulating. Everything around you was alive in vivid color, and you seemed to be walking on air with every step. You probably were so full on life that you had to be reminded to eat.

Now think about a time when things were just the opposite, when you were feeling depressed or lonely. All the food in the world couldn't fill you up, and, no matter how much you ate, you never seemed to be satiated. Both of these scenarios are clear examples of just how important primary food is in our lives.

Primary food is a term I coined to described the non-food-based "foods" that are necessary for maintaining a high quality of life. Primary food is even more necessary to our well-being than the actual food we consume, hence my choosing to label that "secondary food."

That being said, it is also my belief that primary food and secondary food are directly connected. The more primary food you have filling you up in your life, the less secondary food you will need. On the other hand, the more we are dependent on secondary food to fulfill us, the less ability we will have to receive the primary food we're so in need of.

Primary food consists of four main elements: relationships, exercise, career, and spirituality. All of these factors are equally important in and of themselves, but their combination makes up the pillar of your being. When they're all synchronized and contributing positively to your internal state, magic happens.

RELATIONSHIPS

Relationships fulfill an incredibly important need in our lives to connect with other human beings, on both physical and emotional levels. I'm sure that, for most, when the word "relationship" arises, their thoughts go first to the romantic variety. But relationships come in all shapes and sizes, from the one we have with our partner, to the way interactions occur with our friends, to the dynamics that exist between family members.

Unfortunately, many people today are in need of more quality relationships in their lives, having either become isolated after repeated perceived failures or by remaining involved in relationships that no longer serve them and have, instead, started to drag them down.

Take a moment to look truthfully at some of the relationships in your life. How do you feel about them? Are they generally nourishing you, or are they holding you back? You can do this exercise for as many people in your life as you'd like to get the most complete picture.

SERENDIPITOUS MOMENTS

Cultivating Relationships

Tom

I was on my way to a personal development seminar, riding the train early in the morning. I was sitting across from a handsome man, and we kept making eye contact. I usually wouldn't talk to someone on the subway, but I was gearing up for this seminar and feeling very confident. I sat down next to the man and started chatting with him. It turns out that he had previously attended the same seminar that I was headed toward. What are the chances of that? We exchanged numbers, but I was nervous to call him. Then another friend who was doing the seminar with me pushed me to call him to practice the authenticity we were cultivating at this seminar. We hit it off, and we're still together two years later. Wow!

EXERCISE

When it comes to physical activity, it's probably no surprise that most people today simply aren't getting enough of it. The physical body has to be able to burn the food we consume, and it must be in good shape if it's to properly absorb the nutrients and fully experience the benefits of healthy eating.

Even people who do exercise regularly aren't necessarily doing it properly because they don't do enough cross training, instead focusing on one or two exercises that they repeat. For instance, someone who practices yoga every day might not be getting enough cardiovascular exercise, while someone who goes out running every morning might not be training sufficiently for flexibility and strength.

That being said, it is important to remember that each person is different as far as what works for them and their body. Finding exercise that both feels good to you and is enjoyable will help to promote a healthy balance.

What does your exercise routine look like? In which areas could it use improvement?

CAREER

It's amazing what a dramatic effect a person's career can have on their health, for better or for worse. Even when a job or career isn't the right fit for someone, many people are driven to stay due to financial reasons, whether for fear of losing their paycheck or because of lucrative financial benefits. Yet, sometimes, they may also stay longer than they should due to factors like loyalty, longevity, or prestige. Some may even go to the extent of defining themselves as a person wholly by their choice of career.

Of course, there are also plenty of people out there who find great fulfillment in the work they do. For me, it took many years and a number of career changes to finally discover a career that I am passionate about and that resonates with my soul. Today, I love that I get to help people every day, and I feel so lucky to have found my true professional calling.

It's time to get honest with yourself and ask if your career is fulfilling you in a similar way to what I'm talking about. Do you enjoy what you do overall? Do you find that your work is adding to your life or subtracting from it?

Sometimes, it isn't necessarily a career change that's needed but simply some shifts in the daily routine of your job. Maybe you would enjoy what you're doing more if you were working in a different department? Or perhaps simply adding a walk outside into your lunch hour so that you have a break in your day to breathe and reboot could give you the fulfillment you're looking for?

SPIRITUALITY

I heartily encourage everyone to have some kind of spiritual practice. When I say spiritual practice, I mean that you focus on what is spiritual for you as an individual. For some people, this may be the practice they were raised with, while for others they may choose to find a new practice that makes more sense to them, and, for still others, it can be as simple as spending some time outside in nature. The idea is to find what works for you.

How much time do you allocate for some kind of spiritual practice, if any? If you're not a part of an organized or traditional practice, how could you set aside time to connect with yourself on a spiritual level?

As I mentioned previously, primary food connects intimately with secondary food and food cravings, which are a wakeup call that something in life is out of balance. Sometimes that imbalance can be found in diet, but sometimes it's in lifestyle. Some people use food as a reward when they're not treating themselves well enough or when they do not have positive attention from another individual. Can you see how an improvement in primary food would help to reduce your emotionally connected food cravings?

So how does primary food connect with serendipity?

Finding true love and filling myself with primary food was crucial in helping me to slow down, feel deeply satisfied, and allow serendipity to flow. When you're in balance, healthy, and vibrant, serendipity is heightened. The more centered and balanced you are, the more you'll be in the right place at the right time, all the time. When you're in this place, you'll also trust your gut a lot more and notice all of the serendipity already happening in your life instead of speeding past it.

To be centered and balanced means that you have your Circle of Life balanced. Take a look at the following chart. Which areas are strong for you? Which are weak? How can you get support in your weak areas?

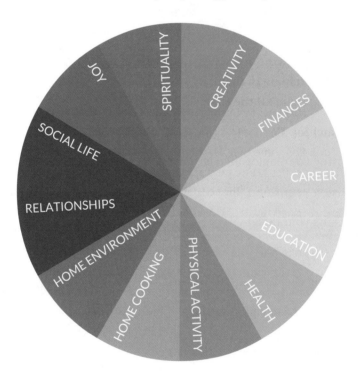

We can only move forward by acknowledging our present condition, both its positive and negative aspects, exactly as it is right now. We have to love ourselves in order to have the courage to step out and make the changes necessary to get us pointed in the direction of our dreams. Self-love means that you feed yourself food that fuels your body, that you engage in only positive relationships, learn to love the work you have or find work you love, do regular exercise you enjoy, and cultivate some sort of spiritual practice that nurtures you.

Lots of activities can take you away from serendipity by numbing your senses and making you more robotic, leading you to conform to the path that society sets out for you rather than your own unique path. Let's do an exercise to see how many of these detracting activities you're engaging in and to what extent.

Rate the following activities on a scale of 0–10, 0 meaning you never participate in them, and 10 meaning that you find yourself doing them all the time:

1. Watching TV

2. Using your laptop all day

3. Using your smart phone

4. Using your tablet

5. Gossiping

6. Eating chemical, artificial junk food

7. Sitting at a computer all day

8. Avoiding exercise

9. Isolating yourself

10. Forcing yourself to socialize when you're exhausted

11. Engaging in petty arguments

Choose the areas you rated highest, meaning you find yourself doing these things all the time, and reduce them by just one hour this week. If you rated many items as a 10, just choose one to reduce, and start there. As you start reducing the time spent on these things, you'll notice it feels good to have more space and calmness, and you'll naturally engage in them less and less.

Now, from the following list, rate each item 0–10, 0 meaning you never do it and 10 meaning you do it all the time:

1. Walking in nature

2. Creative activities, like writing or drawing

3. Having quiet, reflective time

4. Reading

5. Engaging in loving, uplifting conversation

6. Eating lots of fruits and vegetables

7. Moving throughout the day

8. Exercising for 45 minutes 3–5 times a week

9. Connecting with like-minded people

10. Complimenting other people

Choose the area you rated lowest, and commit to spending one more hour at it this week. For instance, if you chose a creative activity, and you don't like to draw, choose some other creative outlet that works for you. It just can't involve technology. The goal here is to unplug from your smart phone and plug in to your smart self. Connect with your core—the stuff that makes up who you really are and keeps you connected to your own personal mission.

Sometimes, in order to bring our primary foods into balance, we must work hard to overcome our fears as we face some very intimidating changes, but it is only by facing those fears and making those changes that we can evolve.

In the next chapter, we're going to continue looking at the concept of balance, specifically with regard to the Chinese ideas of yin and yang and how they can help you to continue on the journey to finding your balance and increasing your serendipity. Are you ready? Let's do this!

4 FINDING THE BALANCE OF YIN & YANG

"The universe is always speaking to us. . . . sending us little messages, causing coincidences and serendipities, reminding us to stop, to look around, to believe in something else, something more."　　　　　　　　*—NANCY THAYER*

We talked a little in chapter 1 about incorporating the Chinese concepts of yin and yang to help maintain balance and invite more serendipity into your daily life.

Another Chinese term, the complex-to-define word "Tao," is most fundamentally described as the balance of all polar energies inherent within nature. When you widen the term into a philosophy, Taoism teaches that if you can strike a balance and harmonize these energies, you will experience peace, order, and justice, not only within yourself, but all around you as well. It also tells us that it is imbalance and chaos which are the true causes of suffering.

Yin and yang energies are the polar opposites of one another. Neither of these energies is inherently good or bad; as each has its place and needs to be expressed. One cannot consistently dominate, nor can one exist independently of the other.

YANG	YIN
Light, solar, daytime, masculine, outward flow, active, analytical, dominant, aggressive, left-brain, right-body.	Dark, lunar, nighttime, feminine, inward flow, restive, intuitive, passive, submissive, right-brain, left-body.

You can experience examples of yin and yang every day, both inside of yourself and out in the world—breathing in and out, birth and death, day and night, the seasonal changes of nature. They are opposites that are defined by their very relationship to one another. Every aspect of life has the potential to express both forms of energy.

So how do these two forces become so out of balance?

For starters, yang is a very dominant energy in today's fast-paced society. The indicators are everywhere; ambitious professions, overbooked schedules, big cities, busy electronics, and continuous global strife are just a few examples of this. Even our western diets tend to be yang-oriented, with an emphasis on meats and heavy foods.

Both yin and yang are energies are meant to be expressed in a moment and should therefore be considered fluid, never set in stone. Yet, often, we are taught to overly identify with one or the other, instead of recognizing that we all have both and that they need to exist in a balanced state. These teachings usually come subversively through those around us, such as friends and family, or from society as a whole.

One easy way to look at it is using the masculine/feminine aspect of yin and yang. Generally speaking, men are typically taught from a young age to be strong, independent, and protective, whereas women are expected to be gentle, soft, and nurturing. Men are naturally more yang, but some men who are always are aggressive and overly macho. Women, on the other hand, are naturally more yin, but some women are always completely submissive and overly effeminate. Of course, it can go the other way, too: there are some highly feminine men who identify more with the yin side and some highly masculine women who identify more with the yang side.

You may be wondering, "What's wrong with men being masculine and women being feminine?" A question to which, of course, the answer is "nothing!" However, it is when an imbalance or repression occurs that problems arise. Although it may not always be apparent, when one side of the energy or another is being repressed, be it passively or with intent, anxiety and angst are the result.

Think about it… Have you ever known someone who was very submissive and who would have benefited from standing up for themselves once in a while? That is an indicator of a yin imbalance. Imbalances can also be created due to external pressures. For example, many women feel the need to fundamentally change who they are to be successful in today's yang work environment, even if that change goes strongly against their naturally yin-oriented energy.

Some signs of excess or unbalanced energy include:

YANG	YIN
Aggressiveness, anxiety, anger, burn out, overly controlling and critical, judgmental, hyperactive, frustrated.	Submissiveness, depression, listlessness, confusion, jealousy, low self-esteem, hopelessness, feeling weak and tired.

Let's look at how these signs of excess energy might manifest in your daily life.

Do you remember a period of time when you felt very in control of your life? You were doing lots of planning and goal setting, getting everything organized, and probably getting a lot done. This is an expression of yang energy, and it probably felt great at the time to be so productive and on top of everything. However, when you're in this state for too long, you will eventually start to burn out, becoming anxious and obsessive.

You've probably also experienced times when you were living life by going with the flow, being carefree, and finding new connections in random moments. This is an expression of yin energy, and it probably felt exciting at the time to let go and revel in the unknown. However, when this energy lasts too long, you might start feeling lost and depressed, finding yourself unable to concentrate or build anything lasting.

You can see through these examples that neither yin nor yang energy is inherently good or bad, each having positive and useful attributes. It is only when an imbalance exists and one side takes over that problems begin to arise. Make sense?

CREATING BALANCE

So the question now becomes how can yin and yang be brought into balance?

It may seem like a highly involved process, but the good news is that you're already exploring the first and most important step by learning all about the differences in the energies and how you can recognize when they are sliding out of alignment.

You don't have to actively try to maintain a balance at first. Instead, begin by observing and deepening your self-awareness. Use the lists of excess energy indicators above to start seeing clearly when your emotional state is indicating an imbalance. One shortcut to spotting an imbalance is to look for any inner negativity or a negative mindset. But even little things, like how much tension you're holding in your body at any given time, are indicators of the balance of yin and yang energy.

Make a list of at least 5 activities you've done in the past 24 hours. This can include projects at work, physical activity, or even watching television. Once you've completed the list, go back and reflect on each activity, and label if it was yin or yang.

Try reflecting on your day in this manner for the next week to see if your current routine is biased toward the yin or the yang. Tracking your experiences like this in your journal is another great way to become more aware of excess energies when they occur. If you find yourself in a negative mindset, take the time to stop and observe exactly what is causing the negativity.

Are you feeling stressed because you are stretching yourself too thin? Try taking some time to step back and reboot, doing some breathing exercises or engaging in activity that will help you to slow down and relax. Are you feeling lost or depressed? Find something to do with intention, like starting a project or taking a brisk walk with an intended destination.

Of course, spotting an imbalance will not always be an easy task; sometimes when it happens it is very subtle and will affect you at a deeper level. By continuing to cultivate mindfulness and awareness in everyday moments, you'll start to have an easier time accurately identifying what is truly happening, and that understanding is key to ultimately righting the imbalance.

When you stay in balance, you will find that conflict melts away. Also, similar to all other emotions and your state of mind, you will find that your inner balance is projected outward. And when you're balanced, you'll attract serendipity and invite synchronistic magic into your life.

Awareness and mindfulness may not seem like goals that are simple to achieve, but they grow through the simultaneous cultivation of stillness, which is what we're going to take a look at in the next chapter, where we go over slowing things down and learning to listen again. Are you with me?

5

CULTIVATING STILLNESS

"I theorize that there is a spectrum of consciousness available to human beings. At one end is material consciousness. At the other end is what we call 'field' consciousness, where a person is at one with the universe, perceiving the universe. Just by looking at our planet on the way back, I saw, or felt, a field consciousness state." —EDGAR MITCHELL

As I mentioned earlier, one of the biggest afflictions of today's society is the level of busy-ness most people are constantly experiencing. We're always on the go and rarely take the time to stop and simply be still for a while. This absolutely applies to our physical bodies, but, even more importantly, this is also true of our minds.

Have you ever found yourself obsessively thinking about something? Maybe it's a problem you're currently experiencing, a project at work, or an event from the past or the future. Your mind refuses to let it go, instead running over it again and again like a broken record. Have you ever found a silly song stuck in your head that you can't seem to shake? Believe it or not, that's yet another symptom of an overactive mind. It seems like our minds are running incessantly.

The mind is an incredible tool that we humans have at our daily disposal. However, that tool becomes a liability when it takes over and starts running the show. Some metaphysical practitioners have even dubbed the term "monkey mind" to describe its unsettled and inconstant nature. Buddha once specifically described the human mind as "being filled with drunken monkeys, jumping around, screeching, chattering, and carrying on endlessly, all clamoring for attention."

So, of course, the idea of calming those monkeys and stilling your mind can seem like a hefty undertaking. But if you want to invite more serendipity into your life and maintain optimal overall well-being, quieting your mind is incredibly important. If you're going to listen to that inner voice of intuition, the one that helps guide you to synchronistic and serendipitous events, you must first be able to hear it. And once the mind is still, you'll wonder at the regular surges of creativity, joy, and peace you will begin to experience.

Believe it or not, stillness is actually our mind's natural state that lies just below the busy mind we've grown accustomed to. So, instead of seeing the stilling of the mind as a task that must be done or an effort that must be expended, see it instead as a reorientation toward stillness and away from the noisy, constantly churning mind.

A number of practices exist to help you through this process. I've included a few here to help you on your journey to inner stillness.

MEDITATION

Meditation is the simple practice of quieting down and turning inward to relax your nervous system and gain mental clarity through sitting in silent stillness. It helps to clear out negativity and quiet the mind, allowing us to experience more clarity and providing us with the ability to tether ourselves to something greater. It also has a very physical effect on the body, engaging the relaxation response in our nervous system, effectively clearing out anxiety and worry.

Meditation is not only one of the oldest techniques for quieting the mind, but it is also one of the most commonly used today. I get really inspired when I meditate, and that's when I get some of my best ideas. I'm sure that, when you think of meditation, the first thing that comes to mind is someone sitting on the floor with their legs crossed, Indian style, hands resting on the knees with palms up and fingers touching. And, granted, sitting can be an awesome way to cultivate stillness. But did you know there are plenty of other ways to meditate that include motion?

Some people enjoy activities such as walking, running, swimming, or biking during their meditative process. Really any simple, repetitive activity can be a great background for meditation—even something like knitting works. Everyone I know who meditates has a different practice, so there is no one right way to do this. Whatever method works best for you, the key is that, during that time, your thoughts are free and that you are taking a break from true thinking, focusing instead on only the present moment and on stilling the mind.

BREATHING PRACTICES

A breathing practice is a typical accompaniment for meditation; however, the two don't necessarily need to go hand in hand. Whether you're at your desk or sitting at home on your couch, regular breathing exercises can help you to calm the mind and release tension from the body.

When you're feeling anxious, there are great breathing techniques you can do to clear out stress. One of the simplest is to practice slow, deep, smooth breathing by inhaling to a count of five or six and then flowing into an exhale of equal length without holding or pausing between the in and the out breath. Another technique, one of my favorites, comes from Integrative Nutrition visiting teacher Andrew Weil, MD. It's called 4–7–8.

Here's how it works:

1. Press the tip of your tongue to the ridge of tissue just above your front teeth. This is said to complete the energy circuit of the world.

2. Let all of the air out through your mouth.

3. Close your mouth, and inhale through the nose quietly to a count of four.

4. Hold your breath to a count of seven.

5. Exhale through the mouth, making a louder noise to a count of eight, pursing your lips and opening your mouth just slightly, pushing the air out while keeping your tongue touching the roof of your mouth.

6. Repeat four breath cycles twice a day or more as tension arises.

This is a great way to manage anxiety and even help you fall asleep. Try it in the morning when you wake up and again before bed to begin with. You will feel amazing and very present in your body afterward.

NEUTRALITY

A huge source of noise in the mind comes from the unconscious patterns and reactions we've developed throughout our lives in response to all of the things that we experience around us. Have you ever noticed how, without any sort of conscious thought, you can find yourself mentally commenting on things like what another person is wearing or the actions of someone around you?

To work on removing this unnecessary chatter, try altering your view of the world so that you're seeing it through completely neutral eyes. This involves ceasing all of the labeling and stereotyping we tend to do without thinking about it, but even more tricky is destroying our natural tendency toward judgment. You'll need to apply this not only to the world around you, but especially to yourself as you learn to disidentify with your thoughts and feelings. When you notice your mind leaping to make a judgment, forcefully think or say the word, "STOP!" to halt it in its tracks. Over time, you'll condition your mind to stop jumping to negativity as a default response to certain situations. When you silence the constant commentary your mind creates, you'll begin to notice just how much quieter everything becomes.

QUIET TIME

The quieter you get, the more you'll hear.

The world outside is never quiet, and today's world is certainly one of noise, both internal and external. Sometimes we use that noise as a screen to distance ourselves from things that we find uncomfortable or unpleasant, the things we don't want to deal with, such as fear and doubts. But quiet time is essential to getting reacquainted with your inner self and finding stillness.

Yet, even when we've turned off all the distractions, there is still noise—the wind blowing outside, the clock in the next room ticking, or even the sound of distant car tires rolling down the pavement. But each of those sounds in itself can be a meditation, a focal point that will provide a momentary escape from the hectic nature of today's world. Is there something around you now that you can focus on? Give it a try.

Some quiet time is a great way to get yourself centered as you begin your daily routine as well as when you find yourself in the middle of a crazy, hectic day. When it feels like everything is chaos around you, take a pause to find 5 minutes of quiet time. Instead of letting the external environment control you and have a negative impact on you, you can control it by keeping a calm mind. How cool is that? It's kind of like a superpower that all humans have. If we all stayed calm and open most of the time, the world would be a much better place.

Sometimes things are meant to happen out of order so that you will appreciate the beauty that arises from disorder and learn to sink into the moment, whatever that moment is. When you can go with the flow and feel gratitude, you will attract serendipity. It's also important to deliberately schedule time to just be with yourself and your thoughts in a place that you find peaceful.

1. **Revisit the meditation and breathing exercises from earlier in this chapter, and commit to practicing them if you haven't already.** These practices can take you out of your head, into your body, and into a place of stillness.

2. **Take a walk in nature.** Walking in nature always reminds me that I can just be. I don't have to be active and engaged, and just being in the void is so productive because it supports creativity by refueling you.

3. **Get a massage.** Being in this state of receiving is a great way to sink into the void. Receiving a massage is the opposite of engaging your mind. It's one of the few activities where you're actually supposed to quiet your mind and relax, which is very healing.

4. **Take a hot bath.** Baths engage the nervous system's relaxation response, putting us into a deep state of bliss and guiding us away from our busy minds. Take one at least twice a week to stay connected to yourself and the universe and to bring more serendipity into your life.

5. **Stretch.** Stretching every morning is a great way to activate your body. Notice what feels good and what's bothering you, and give yourself some attention. When you're in tune with your body, you're in tune with the universe.

6. **Practice yoga.** Practicing yoga is an amazing way to get out of your mind and into your body. The hour or so that you might practice is an amazing void in itself, since you truly have nowhere to go and nothing to do except be present. Practicing yoga is one of my favorite ways to bring more serendipity into my life.

Even as busy as I get with my role at IIN, I, too, make sure to schedule it into my calendar—times of just nothing. Space lets you enjoy simple pleasures and engages all of your senses, allowing you to become aware of your thoughts in that quiet time and in the present. It is when you become numb to simple pleasures that you shut out synchronicity and serendipity. But when you're aware of and grateful for those simple sensory pleasures, you're saying "yes" to synchronicity. We're going to take a look in the next chapter at awareness and gratitude and how they can draw more serendipity into your life. Are you with me?

SERENDIPITOUS MOMENTS

Becoming Still & Grateful

Rachel

As I left yet another job in the restaurant industry, part of a three-year slump I couldn't seem to pull out of, I found myself asking the ultimate question: Where was I really heading in life? I ended up in a small corner bookshop where the bright glowing cover of a book on gratitude caught my eye. Little did I know, this book would change my life forever.

As I began to take time out of each day to learn how to be still, silent, and grateful in each area of my life, my life began to respond and thrive like never before. My consultation business began to take off. I found mentors in unexpected people. I received a free education through an amazing job with an artistic firm. I became motivated to set boundaries that were aligned with my intentions, and I found great peace in deeper personal connections.

As I acknowledged beauty, more beauty showed up. Laughter and movement became my best friends, which could fend off any creeping doubt or fear, and love became my new life strategy.

6 AWARENESS & GRATITUDE

"At times, our own light goes out and is rekindled by a spark from another person. Each of us has cause to think with deep gratitude of those who have lighted the flame within us." —Albert Schweitzer

The next step in the process of creating more serendipity in your life is twofold: first, recognizing how often you're already experiencing, and second, learning to be appreciative and grateful for those experiences. I can't stress just how important these steps are in opening the gates to so many more serendipitous and positive experiences in your life.

Let me share with you a series of experiences I had recently while on a little getaway with my partner in Boston. We had decided to make a visit to the beach, despite the coolness of the day, and we really wanted to take a dip in the water, although we were sure it was likely too chilly for that. I noticed a guy who had just come out of the water, and without a thought I jumped off of our towel to ask him if it was warm or cold. As I asked my question, the woman with him chimed in and said that I had asked the right person—it turns out the guy was a triathlete and had just measured the water temperature, which was 55 degrees Fahrenheit. Out of all of the people I could have asked, I'd felt compelled to pop right up and ask him. Pretty amazing, huh?

Then, later that same day in Boston, as we were getting out of the car to stretch our legs, I saw a young couple walk by out of the corner of my eye who looked slightly lost. For some reason, I decided to approach them; I do things like this a lot because I follow my gut instincts. I simply asked if I could help them find something. As it turned out, they were looking for the exact same restaurant that we had made reservations for earlier in the day, so I was able to easily provide them with directions. Even stranger was the fact that we weren't even near the restaurant, which made this interaction completely "random" and ultimately synchronistic. I use quotes around the word random because I don't believe that anything is truly random; everything is intentional, guiding us to our next step.

Can you see how the concept of reciprocity was at work during that day? I had wanted some information earlier in the day, and it came right to me. In turn, I was then able to help someone out later in the day. It's all about the cycle of giving and receiving and expressing gratitude throughout the process.

Serendipity appears in both small and large events, and both are equally important in creating a healthy, happy life. Don't let yourself go into comparison mode. Even if your occurrence seems less significant or impactful than someone else's, it's still a testament to the power of serendipity, and celebrating even the smallest happenings will bring more of it into your life. We humans usually try to understand things in very black and white terms—big or small, important or not important. What we miss when we do this are all of the beautiful shades of gray, and the magic of serendipity certainly comes in many shades.

Have you ever noticed how wonderful children are at appreciating magic? Unfortunately, as adults, we are more likely to constantly be taking stock, with questions such as "How important is this?" or "How much is that worth?" But it's a mistake to try to quantify things when we're talking about serendipity. Instead, just letting them happen and appreciating every little instance will bring the greatest reward because whatever you're focusing on will grow, and you'll find that all of the little things will turn into big things.

SERENDIPITOUS MOMENTS

Practicing Awareness

Christina

Even when we make an incorrect turn while driving or are annoyed by that person who is driving slowly, it's important, and there's a reason for it.

Breathe and embrace the moment. Say to yourself, "This is for my protection," or you can also ask, "What can I learn, recognize, or appreciate in this situation?"

The great things that happen to me personally are when I think about something that I would like to do. Then something happens, and I find that information through a stranger or a person I know, not by asking them, but it just comes up in conversation. So amazing! Or I think about visiting someone, and they happen to call me, whether it's my sister in Florida or my friend in California. Life is good, and I am grateful for this universal gift!

I want you to think back to one serendipitous incident that happened recently that you really took notice of, be it big or small. Maybe it was as simple as running into someone who you were really missing and wanted to see for an important reason, or perhaps the person next to you at the gym struck up a conversation with you that led you to your dream job.

One serendipitous event that happened to me in the last year was:

Now, I want you to use this exercise as a reminder to start noticing when serendipity and synchronicity occur on a daily basis. Keep your small notebook with you, and make notes when these events happen. The more you can begin to call awareness to the fact that serendipity is ever-present in your life, the more you'll be able to notice immediately when something is off or when serendipitous events are not happening, and you'll become more comfortable with signaling the universe to send you more.

Sometimes, those signals don't even have to be completely intentional. When I moved into my home, the road wasn't paved yet, and it was really difficult to drive on. I joked one day that it would be nice if the neighboring town paved the road. Guess what? I woke up the next morning, and the road was paved. It may seem like a leap of faith sometimes, but this stuff really works. All of those small synchronicities quickly add up, and the result is an incredible amount of joy in your life. And when you have that joy, you become a part of the snowball effect as you, in turn, send it out to the universe and find it increasingly coming back to you.

Unfortunately, most people often get so absorbed in the minutia of their daily lives that they stop appreciating the simple magic that's happening all around them. When we don't acknowledge serendipitous events or brush them off as nothing, we lessen our ability to experience them. Alternately, it's when we appreciate and celebrate them that more naturally comes our way. Despite the frequency with which I experience serendipity in my own life, I'm still always fascinated and amazed when it happens to me. I don't bother getting too caught up in the "why" either, because you won't always know why, and really you don't need to know. The universe works in mysterious ways; just celebrate it, and be grateful.

SERENDIPITOUS MOMENTS

Acknowledging Serendipity

Maria

I got waitlisted for an opportunity to travel to Brazil for a program that I really, really wanted to get into. Because I was on that waitlist, I ended up being recruited for a brand-new opportunity in Argentina that wasn't even an option for people applying to the original program I was going after. I accepted the second, serendipitous opportunity and ended up having a much better experience than I would have had in Brazil. I made lifelong friends and had one of the best years of my life. I love when disappointment leads to something amazing.

Synchronicity and serendipity are like muscles in the body—you have to continue to talk about them and use them if you want to keep them active and effective in your life. Once you become aware of the magic going on in your life and everything you already have, it's time to get grateful. Gratitude might even be more important than awareness, but since you need to be aware to be grateful, cultivating awareness comes first.

To move to the next level in your career, relationships, health, or spirituality, it's vital to be aware of, and grateful for, what you already have. Awareness and gratitude are the foundation for personal growth, and they are really what will propel you to the next level. A lot of people totally miss this piece and wonder why they are not expanding in their lives. More often than not, it's because they're lacking in awareness of, and gratitude for, everything they already have. It's the process of acknowledging what you have and expressing gratitude for it through writing or talking with someone that automatically creates room for more growth, success, or whatever you're envisioning for yourself.

What can you recognize that you're grateful for right now? Use your instinct, and write down the first five things that come to you. They could be as simple as a soft breeze on your face, your health, or a meaningful relationship in your life.

1.

2.

3.

4.

5.

Now, let's expand on that exercise. I want you to get very specific with each category of primary food—career, relationships, exercise, and spirituality—as well as secondary food. Complete the following exercise to reflect on your life up until this point and to think about the future. This will help you to gain insight on what is currently working for you and what is not, what you're grateful for at this moment, which areas you would like to change and what changes you can be making in the present, where you would like to see yourself in the future, and what your ultimate goals are.

Career

What kind of work are you currently doing? What does your current work-day look like?

What parts of your work are you grateful for? What parts would you like to change? How does your work make you feel?

What other kinds of work would you like to be doing? How would it change what your ideal day looks like?

Where would you like to see yourself professionally in 1 year? 5 years? 10 years?

Relationships

What are the most important relationships in your life currently? How do they make you feel?

Which relationships or aspects of your current relationships are you grateful for?

What kind(s) of relationships or aspects of relationships do you feel are missing from your life?

How would you like your relationship to be in 1 year? 5 years? 10 years?

Exercise

What is your current exercise routine? How does it make you feel?

How are you currently working to improve or change your exercise routine?

What would you like to accomplish with exercise, and where would you like to be with regard to physical fitness in 1 year from now? 5 years? 10 years?

Spirituality

What spiritual practice were you raised with? In what ways did it meet or not meet your needs?

What is your current spiritual practice? In what ways does it meet or not meet your needs?

Where would you like your spiritual practice to be in 1 year? 5 years? 10 years?

Food

Describe your current diet with regard to what you consume on a regular basis, what your priorities are, and what you like or don't like about it:

What is your ultimate goal with your diet? Is it to be healthier? Feel better physically?

In what ways would you like to change your diet in the immediate future?

What would your ideal diet look like in the long term? What would it accomplish for you?

Completing this exercise will help you to feel grateful for what you already have and to create goals and intentions for how you want your life to be. Getting grateful will begin increasing your positive energy, both internally and externally as what you're sending out into the universe. Getting clear on what you want for your future will clarify for you exactly what you're asking for when that positive energy comes back around.

SERENDIPITOUS MOMENTS

Experiencing Gratitude

Merita

I had been working as a Health Coach for three years, and I was excited about the new opportunities that brought—freedom and following my life-long passion.

One day I went for a run; it was the first day of spring, and I felt such gratitude. We had just moved into our new home. My sons were healthy, and I was in a loving marriage. This was the first time I was not listening to any music, just feeling the air and enjoying the view of the mountains. Everything was going so well, but somehow I got this feeling that there was something missing in my career.

I had worked in the nutrition science field for the past 20 years, and I felt that I wanted to have more of it in my life again. I started making a mental list of what that would be: an English-speaking workplace outside of my home, an ethical company, and working on scientific materials. With each point that I listed, I felt that I was breathing deeper and with more ease. I left this list "with the mountains," like I usually say, not thinking more about it, and continued my run home.

The next day, I got a phone call from a headhunter asking if I would consider working for a company developing medication to help children with rare genetic diseases.

My first question was how they knew I was looking, since it hadn't even been 24 hours since I got this clarity. She said, "I just looked at our communication from 2011 and thought that you would be the perfect match for this job." I had to sit down. I didn't believe it. It felt so right.

Gratitude, honesty, and intention will always overrule rational thinking. Letting go of what you're "supposed" to do and listening to what you are meant to do will always lead you to the right path.

GRATITUDE, LIFE, & DEATH

If you want to increase the synchronicity and serendipity in your life even more, try writing one thank-you note every day to someone who has helped you or just to someone you appreciate. Writing these even once a week or once a month is a great start. It's funny how, once you start writing, it's hard to stop—you'll get addicted and want to do it more and more often. Just don't get stuck in perfection paralysis. It's okay to write thank-you notes on plain paper; your spelling does not have to be perfect, and your notes can be short and sweet. Writing gratitude lists and thank-you letters will greatly improve your career, relationships, and general success in life, and will increase feelings of wholeness and oneness. Who doesn't want that?

Every little bit of gratitude is important, of course, but, above all else, the most necessary and basic thing to be grateful for is life itself. This might surprise you, but a lot of people are really preoccupied with and worry about death so much that they forget they should be living their life to the fullest every day. Another aspect of this fear is that when people get very old and sick, we can have a hard time letting them pass on to their next phase of existence and instead try to keep them alive through artificial methods. When someone is in pain and not able to really live, we should let him or her pass. It's difficult to accept, but it's a natural progression that doesn't have to be taboo.

When I was five or six years old, my parents had a friend named Olga who had been sick for a long time. When Olga eventually passed away, my parents didn't have a babysitter, so they took me to the funeral. I remember my mom telling me as we were getting ready to go, "She was very sick and now, you know, Aunt Olga has gone to Heaven," and I was like, "Sounds good to me." I know that might sound insensitive, but if someone is suffering, I think it's best to feel gratitude for the amazing life they've lived and let them pass on to their next stage or just simply let them stop suffering. Mourning is a natural process, but fear about death is a conscious choice.

As we arrived at the funeral, I noticed that everyone was crying, and as a child I was thinking to myself, "I don't understand. She was sick, and now she died and went to Heaven. Isn't this good?" She was so sick for so long, and, every time I'd seen her, she was in so much pain. So, as I looked around me, I was trying to grasp what death was and why people were freaking out about it so much.

I had a very different experience when the father of my close friend David passed away from cancer. His passing was considered a good thing by his loved ones because, although he had lived a good and full life, he was only suffering in the end. It was fascinating to speak with David about how the family gathered together after his father's passing. Despite their accepting outlook regarding their father's passing, none of David's siblings were prepared to spend time with the body after he'd passed because they were too freaked out by the process on a basic level. David himself, on the other hand, was much more comfortable with it, thanks to his background as a physician.

I hope these stories shift your mindset around life and death and show you what a great learning experience they can both be, helping you to bring more gratitude and awareness into your life. We must release what's ready to be released, including people, to make room for serendipity. If you have a mindset of gratitude, it releases the tension you might have around death and allows you to live a life full of love and synchronicity. I have a lot of admiration for people who can be present with what's real, even if it might be considered unpleasant or difficult to accept by society, and who show gratitude for what is and what was. Once you make the shift to this mindset, synchronicity will come easily to you, and this understanding will help you define the ways you connect to the universe and all the powers that exist within it.

7 CONNECTING
WITH THE
WHOLE

"It would be well, perhaps, if we were to spend more of our days and nights without any obstruction between us and the celestial bodies, if the poet did not speak so much from under a roof, or the saint dwell there so long. Birds do not sing in caves, nor do doves cherish their innocence in dovecots."

—HENRY DAVID THOREAU

We just talked in the last chapter about learning to pay attention to the small pleasures in life, and that relates the topic we're going to look at now: connection.

Connection—beginning with loved ones and family, the world, and up to the infinite scale of a higher power—is incredibly important. So many of us are so busy rushing through life trying to cross things off our to-do lists that we completely miss out on these connections. This pattern ultimately leads to anxiety, depression, and unhappiness.

COMMUNITY & CONNECTION

What's more important to you: your work or your friendships? Maintaining a perfect diet or enjoying a night out with your partner? Exercising five days a week or making time for your spiritual practice?

Everyone wants to enjoy life. Yet, so often, we put our priority on the former. We choose work, maintaining a perfect diet, and hitting the gym every day over our friendships, our love relationships, and our spiritual center.

Don't get me wrong; all of these things are very important, but it's more important to be balanced and enjoy your life. If you're always busy, rigid, refuse to ever indulge in rich food or skip a day of exercise, you might miss out on a lot of bonding time with friends and family. Maintaining this delicate balance will not only make life more enjoyable, but it will make it more doable. We're not wired to be productive all of the time. We need time off in order to reset so we can come back to 100%.

A good rule of thumb is to use the 90/10 principle: 90% of the time, eat the food you know is best for you, exercise often, and try to live with intention. The other 10% of the time, do whatever you feel like doing. For example, with food, let's say you have 21 meals in a week, or three meals a day. A little over two of those meals would equal 10%, so, for those two meals, you can allow yourself to have whatever you want.

I used to work at a health food store, and I would see people meticulously reading labels and buying only the best organic ingredients. What's interesting is that, although these people would literally spend hours grocery shopping, when I actually talked with them, I would discover that some of them were still feeling terrible, physically and emotionally, and that there wasn't a lot of synchronicity happening in their lives.

Then I would go to the movie theater next door and see people eating popcorn and candy and drinking soda, and they seemed so happy and healthy. Why? Because they were connecting with their loved ones, relaxing, and allowing synchronicity to flow freely.

It seems counterintuitive, but when we're having fun, we produce the happy hormone, serotonin, which wipes out cortisol, the stress hormone. The more you engage in activities that feel good, the more serotonin you produce, which means you feel anxious and are less likely to experience digestive issues, weight gain, and other undesirable health problems.

CONNECTING WITH FRIENDS AND FAMILY

Connecting with other people is one of the most important components in bringing more serendipity into your life. How are you doing in the area of relationships and support from friends and family?

A lot of people find it hard to ask for help, especially in today's society where everyone is expected to be autonomous and perfectly self-sufficient, like machines. We're often afraid to respond to the question, "How are you?" with anything besides "fine" or "good." When you're honest with other people, it reminds them that you're a vulnerable human being who needs support and gives them subconscious permission to be honest about their own needs, too. This is pretty cool, because it means you can help others by asking for help yourself.

Your challenge: For the next week, when someone asks how you are, avoid the words "fine" and "good." Challenge yourself to be honest and say how you're really doing. Maybe you really are feeling good, but use a different word like "energetic" or "inspired." Or, if you're not feeling so well, be honest, and tell them.

Remember, no one can do everything on their own. We all need help. It's so important to talk through what's going on for you and open yourself up for support. When you're feeling loved and connected, you're much more likely to attract synchronistic situations and events.

If you find it difficult to stay connected to your friends and family, or if your loved ones are far away, try scheduling two to three dates with them every week, even if it has to be over the phone or using a tool like FaceTime or Skype. It doesn't replace in-person connection, but it's a heart-warming alternative.

However, it's also essential to build a community locally so you'll have people geographically close by to connect with. Find an organization you want to be a part of, or even a Meetup group, so you can connect with like-minded people, which will not only allow you to feel supported, but will also let you be supportive, which is equally important.

Take action: Call or email three people and set up a date. Write down their names and when you are going to connect with them.

1.

2.

3.

How would you currently rate yourself in the area of connection on a scale of 0–10, 0 being you don't connect with others at all, and 10 being you feel very connected? Make a note of this number in your journal, and after 30 days of sticking to your dates with friends and family, revisit that number to see how it has improved. It has been scientifically proven that it takes 30 days to form new habits and mental grooves. You're going to notice how much better you feel when you're connected, and you'll see improvements in all areas of your life, even those that seem unrelated.

SERENDIPITOUS MOMENTS

Family Connection

Andrew

I had just moved from the Upper East Side of New York City into an exciting new apartment in the Financial District. Upon arrival on move-in day, the doorman asked me if my sister lived in the building, since there was another Rendrick (my last name) in his records. My sister did not live there, but I later found out that my cousin, Jackson, whom I had not kept in touch with, lived there. He's from a side of the family that I had always wanted to spend more time with, but due to work and location, it never happened. Serendipity brought us together, and we became great friends.

CONNECTING WITH THE PLANET

Once you're feeling connected to your family and friends, you want to start thinking about how you can connect with the whole. Do you feel connected on a global level? Even though you're a small part of the whole, it's cool to see how you fit into the big picture. Notice how important you are while also realizing that there's so much at play that's bigger than you. What comes to mind when you think of the big picture?

I love donating to causes that I feel passionate about, like education, because it make me feel connected to the world. Even if you donate just one dollar to a cause you believe in, you're going to feel amazing and bring a lot more synchronicity into your life just through that seemingly small action. When you acknowledge how huge the world is, the universe acknowledges you as an important piece. Energy flows through you, and more serendipity shows up in your life.

A lot of people get stuck around donating because they feel like they need to be wealthy to do so, and that's not true. Think about what you spend your money on—maybe $5 lattes or $11 juices. If you skipped something like this just one time, you could donate a few dollars to a great cause and make a difference in the world. Every little bit counts.

The great part is that when you donate even a small amount, it comes back to you tenfold. When you put out into the universe that you're ready to support others, the universe brings you abundance. It's a natural flow of give and take.

Volunteering your time is also a great way to feel connected to something larger than yourself. You don't have to spend hours every week. Just one day a month can go a long way over time.

Even if you're not volunteering, and you're getting paid for what you do, if your work is in line with your life's mission and values, you will be of great service. Reevaluate your work every six months or more so, and ask yourself how you're serving the world and how you're serving yourself. When you remain in the service mindset, you attract a lot of abundance and serendipity.

Take some quiet time alone with your journal to reflect on the following questions, and write down your responses:

In what ways do you feel connected to the world? What makes you feel connected to people in different countries?

Do you feel like you live in a bubble? Why or why not? What makes you feel isolated?

In what ways do you currently contribute to the whole? Do you travel and do work with people in low-income areas? Do you donate? Do you volunteer your time?

What can you do to contribute more and affect people on a basic level? Could you take time to ask the sales clerk how they are and really mean it? Could you smile at a stranger?

What's one cause you feel strongly about? Is there anything stopping you from donating a small amount to that cause?

How can you volunteer some of your time to serve others?

What else can you do today to help you connect to the whole?

CONNECTING WITH A HIGHER POWER

We touched briefly on the subjects of spirituality and religion when we talked earlier in the book about primary food, but now I'd like to dive deeper. Spirituality is an integral part of attracting serendipity. Some people are very religious, and others are very resistant and skeptical about words like "God." Wherever you fall on this spectrum, it's okay. The only thing I will recommend is that you feel a connection to some kind of higher power, whether you call it the divine, the universe, Mother Nature, God, or something completely different. The reality is that all of those terms aim to describe the same phenomenon—the underlying meaning and energy that we feel connecting all living things—and it is the same phenomenon, the same flow, that we step into to find serendipity.

People can sometimes have very rigid ideas about what exactly "spirituality" means, but, in truth, it's an incredibly dynamic word. For instance, one fantastic way to nourish your spirituality that is often overlooked is to spend time in nature. Take the time to look around you at all the beauty in living things, at the clouds during the day and the stars at night. Breathe deeply, and feel gratitude for Mother Nature surrounding you. Being in nature really helps put things in perspective: We're all on a ball spinning in an endless universe. When we stay in tune with Mother Nature and the natural rhythms, we naturally attract more serendipity. Makes sense, right?

Another important part of spiritual practice that many people don't consider is the ripple effect that a belief in something greater than yourself can have on your perspective in life. Be it a supreme being or the combined energy of the universe, the connection and support that is received from the understanding that something higher than yourself exists is unparalleled. It provides an ever-present source from which to seek help and answers when you're struggling.

Take action: Let's dig into your beliefs surrounding spirituality. Spend 5–10 minutes responding to the following questions on a new page in your journal:

1. What are five words that come to mind when you hear the word spirituality?

2. What do you think of people who are religious?

3. What influence does your upbringing and your past have on how you feel about religion today?

4. What role does spirituality currently play in your life?

5. Do you feel like your current relationship with spirituality is your choice, or is it ingrained in you from childhood?

When you feel like you have completely addressed those questions, start on a new page, and answer the following:

1. How would a deeper spiritual practice support you?

2. What specific changes might you see in your life if you felt more connected to the whole in some way? A more aligned career? More loving, supportive relationships? More abundance?

3. What is one action step you can take to improve your spiritual connection? What does that look like for you?

Spirituality is a big topic, and we could spend a lot of time on it, but I want you to start with those questions and see how it goes. It will be helpful to cultivate some form of spirituality in your life if you haven't already, which is to say any relationship with something higher than yourself. As you start shifting your attention to this area, the action steps you need to take will become clear. Maybe you're religious and place your faith in a single supreme being, or maybe you simply believe in karma and the energy of the universe. Either one is great and will be helpful in guiding you toward more serendipity in your life.

Start small as you work to build your spiritual practice and see what feels right for you. This is easy to determine because you will naturally want to do more of what feels good, and when you feel great, you'll not only attract more serendipity, but you'll begin to find you have less room in your life for old junk—physical or emotional—that no longer serves you. Sound good?

8

LETTING GO AND MAKING ROOM

"Respect yourself enough to walk away from anything that no longer serves you, grows you, or makes you happy."
                                                              —ROBERT TEW

Everyone has a story.

It's a story about their past and how they came to be the person they are today, and it includes both the good and the bad. While there's no doubt that the building blocks of our past can be important, it becomes a problem when we let the past dictate the present or the future.

We're all born as blank canvases that inevitably pick up physical and emotional baggage as we move through life, but who we are does not need to be a reflection of that baggage. Opportunities for growth and change exist in every part of our lives, calling us to release all of the unnecessary junk we're carrying around.

In this chapter, I'll show you how to let go of that junk to make room for more serendipity in your life.

There are really two kinds of junk: physical and mental. Of course, physical junk is typically easy to spot—a refrigerator that's overflowing with leftovers that have gone bad, a closet with clothes that are ill-fitting or worn out, or a desk where we can't find important papers because it's so cluttered and there's no filing system—are all obvious examples of physical junk.

We also have mental and emotional junk. This includes old habits, patterns, beliefs, and stories we've been holding on to for years. Many of us have these negative tapes that repeatedly play in our heads. These tapes contain messages like "I'm not good enough," or "I'll never have a career I love," or "No one will ever love me." These are examples of limiting beliefs, stories we've told ourselves based on our experiences, and they are perfect examples of emotional junk that we have to get rid of in order to reach our full potential. As long as you're holding on to those old stories about yourself, you'll have a difficult time making room for serendipity to flow in your life.

Clearing out all your mental clutter can seem daunting, whereas clearing out physical clutter seems much more doable. The good news is:

You can start with clearing your physical clutter! This will start positive momentum in your life that will make letting go of emotional clutter much easier. Not only that, but your outer world reflects your inner world, and when you start making changes to one, the other naturally starts changing as well. So when you start clearing up your physical clutter, you'll notice that you naturally start releasing mental/emotional clutter.

CLEAR YOUR PHYSICAL CLUTTER

Start with one area of your apartment or house, and clean it up this week. You can start small with a confined area, like under your bathroom sink, or you can choose to get a little more ambitious and tackle an entire room. Your workspace and your closet are two especially important areas to conquer. As far as your workspace goes, it's very helpful to keep this space clear of clutter and to add some inspiring items like photos of loved ones and uplifting quotes. When it comes to your closet, go by the rule that if you haven't used or worn something in more than a year, donate it if it's still usable, or throw it out if it's not. A great trick to keep track of this is to pick a memorable starting point, like the first of the year, and turn all of your hangers backward. When you wear something, replace the hanger in its usual forward-facing direction. The hangers that are backward after a year are items that you're no longer using that can be given away.

Just as important as *clearing* your space is making sure that you're not filling up that space with more clutter! Make a commitment to stop collecting random trinkets and other things that fill up your space. The outer reflects the inner, and a cluttered space leads to a cluttered mind. You won't believe how much better you'll feel when your home and work spaces are clean and clear. Just be careful not to overwhelm yourself with the process. Break it down, and take it one small step at a time. Even if you start with just one shelf or one drawer, you'll notice how much better you feel after you get it cleaned up, and you'll want to keep going and clear out even more.

Once you're satisfied with the decluttering, learn to make it a monthly ritual. Every month, set aside a day to clear out junk. Over time, watch your mind become clearer, and watch yourself become more aligned with your purpose. You'll also find yourself more motivated to invest energy into your goals and to spend more time doing things you love. Another cool thing that happens when we start throwing things away is that we often start losing any excess weight naturally. An overstuffed closet really does translate to physical excess and discomfort in your body. Try it out! And once you're clear of excess physical and emotional baggage, you'll naturally increase your ability to experience serendipity.

> **Take action: Right now, mark one day per month that you'll use only for clearing out junk. Use your daily planner or your digital calendar. It's good to choose the same day every month and stick to it. If you can only set aside an hour or two, that's okay! Just take the first step.**

CLEAR YOUR MENTAL/ EMOTIONAL CLUTTER

Now that you've conquered your physical junk, the next step is to tackle your mental junk. The majority of this junk is composed of the stories that have been engrained in us from our childhood experiences or that we've made up about ourselves later in life, sometimes as a direct result of those same childhood experiences. Maybe your parents gave you the idea that it's really difficult to make money or that it's bad to make money. Or perhaps a relative taught you that it's dangerous to accept love. Everyone has a different story, but the common thread we all share is that most of us have at least one early childhood experience that negatively and strongly impacted us, something that we need to release in order to move forward in our lives.

I'll share with you a story from my own life: In first grade, my teacher asked me why I always put my hand up when she asked a question. I felt embarrassed and ashamed, since she said it in front of the entire class, so I never put my hand up again, and that stifled my ability to speak up and have my voice be heard. It also changed my entire learning experience and possibly stunted it. But I was the one who actively chose to harbor the misguided belief that I shouldn't speak up for all those years. Had I released my baggage and kept on raising my hand, I might have learned more instead of just feeling stupid for asking too many questions. Asking questions is critical to personal growth.

To move forward in my life and to keep expanding my knowledge, I had to unlearn the belief that it's not okay to ask questions and that it makes you look silly if you do. I did this by working with mentors and opening myself to authentic relationships with other people. I opened my heart and got curious. Now, in my adult life, I've finally gotten back to my childlike self by asking a lot of questions and allowing myself to be really curious about other people. That's how you can learn a lot!

I'll give you another personal example: By the time I got to 4th grade, I was failing school. I was doing my own type of computer programming on paper and trying to figure out a secret code. My mother was getting really angry with me for not passing school because I was working on this system. She would hover over my shoulder, making sure I was doing what I needed to do for class, and she was the last person I wanted to disappoint. I was really interested in creating this brilliant new computer system, but I was boxed in by standardized tests and expectations from my family.

Since my mom was always nagging me, and I was afraid I would disappoint her, I developed a story that this is how all women are. For a good part of my adult life, I automatically associated every woman I met with being overbearing and nagging. It's not necessarily true that every woman is going to hover over me or that I need to be fearful that I'll disappoint everyone; that's just a story I told myself as a result of the experience with my mother.

We pick up all of this baggage throughout our lives, but we're not necessarily aware that we're carrying it. We think it's *just the way things are*. The truth is that we have a choice: We can become conscious that it exists and decide to work on expelling it, or we can keep on pretending that this is just the way things are.

When a person keeps accumulating false and limiting beliefs without working to release them, they will eventually shrivel up and shut down. In many cases, this baggage will even ultimately manifest as mental and/or physical illness. The bottom line is that we are the inventors of our own behavior. Until a shift in our attention occurs, and we get active in deciding how we want to live, we will continue to run on autopilot, and our baggage will greatly influence the way we act.

Let's take another look at the five primary food areas that you've previously examined in other chapters to determine where you might be carrying emotional baggage that you're not aware of. We'll first examine what your current story might be, and then we'll determine what your new truth should look like.

Relationships

Relationships are probably one of the biggest topics in the area of baggage. Perhaps an incident in your childhood where you felt unloved by your mother or father has resulted in your feeling undeserving of love as an adult. Or maybe you find yourself repeatedly in relationships with dynamics that are very similar to the ones that existed between your parents. It's incredibly easy to fall into patterns of your own that resemble those which were imprinted onto you throughout your childhood years, at vital times when all of your mental habits and ways of thinking were still developing.

Take action: Acknowledge your relationship patterns and their possible origins. Ask yourself the following questions, and write down your responses:

1. What is the biggest hurdle that I struggle with most frequently in relationships?

2. Do I always go for the same "types"? Who in my life growing up was most like that?

3. What beliefs do I have about love that might be keeping me from an ideal relationship with a person who loves me?

4. Do I love myself? Have I acknowledged that I must love myself deeply before I can attract an aligned partner?

5. Do I believe I deserve unconditional love for just being myself rather than for what I do or create in the world?

After writing thorough responses to these questions, answer the following on a fresh page in your journal:

1. In what ways can I learn to love myself more so that other people can love me more as well?

2. What characteristics does my ideal partner have? Why are these characteristics "ideal" to me? Try to go beyond the surface, and dig deep for your answers.

3. What junk do I have in my life that I need to clear out to make space for my ideal partner?

Changing any limiting, negative beliefs about relationships is an important step, but it's equally, if not more important, to first establish the belief that you deserve love and respect. Being loved, by a partner, friends, or family, is a birthright that every person should experience continuously throughout their lives.

Money

This is another big area in which people tend to carry a lot of emotional baggage. Many people have stories about money, yet few of them realize it. Explore this for yourself, and do some journaling on the subject. What was your financial situation as a child? What kind of negative beliefs might you have acquired growing up? Do you currently feel like money is scarce in your life or that there's not enough to go around? These beliefs might seem inconsequential, but they actually have the power to change everything.

> **Take action: Dive deep into your own money story. Get curious instead of judgmental, and be honest with yourself. Ask yourself the following questions, and write the answers in your journal:**
>
> 1. What was I taught about money as a child?
>
> 2. What do I think of people who make a lot of money?
>
> 3. If I'm not making the money I want or need to be making, what might be stopping me?
>
> 4. Who has the power here? Have I given my power away? To whom?
>
> 5. In which situations do I feel best in the area of money? When do I feel at ease about money?

Take a moment to examine what you've written for limiting beliefs and negativity. When you find it, write down a statement that will reverse that negativity and replace those beliefs with positive affirmations, statements like "I attract abundance of all kinds" or "There is plenty to go around, and I deserve abundance."

We have the ability to create our own lives, but in order to do that we have to get very clear about what it is that we want. To create what you want in the area of money, you need to get really specific about your ideal scenario in terms of the way you feel about money on an emotional level and the logistics of what you need to create that reality.

Create an intention by outlining your ideal money situation. Write down responses to the following questions.

1. How would my life change if I were making what I needed or wanted to make?

2. How could earning more money change the lives of others?

3. What's one step I can take to improve my financial situation? When will I take that step?

Spirituality

Plenty of people develop roadblocks in their lives when it comes to the subject of spirituality, which is not surprising, since spirituality is something that can become a big part of a person's life early on. However, as we get older, and we're able to make decisions for ourselves, we don't always find that what we were taught to believe when we were young still works for us as an adult. There are even some people who have had extreme experiences with spirituality in their youth—either good or bad—that are affecting their present-day perceptions.

Take action: Let's get into your story as it pertains to spirituality. Answer the following questions in your journal:

1. What role does spirituality currently play in your life? Do you feel like this is by choice, or was it engrained in you by your upbringing?

2. What do you think of people who are religious?

3. How do you believe the way you were raised affects your views on religion and spirituality today?

Write for 5–10 minutes or longer, then start on a new sheet of paper, and answer the following questions:

1. How would a deeper spiritual practice support you?

2. What specific changes might you see in your life if you felt more connected to the whole in some way? A more aligned career? More loving, supportive relationships? More abundance?

3. What is one action step you can take to improve your spirituality? What does that improvement look like for you?

Spirituality can be a very deep and complex topic, which is why it isn't surprising that some may find it confusing or even off-putting. But it's important to find your own way to connect with the greater powers in the universe and work through any residual issues you may be carrying in that area.

Physical Activity

So many people I know think that exercise is all about highly visible and immediate results and that they have to exercise for multiple hours each day, five days a week in order to see those results. But the problem is that they often get so tripped up by those beliefs that that they don't end up exercising at all! The truth is that a little exercise is better than none, so let's get moving.

Take action: It's time to debunk your exercise myths. Answer the following questions in your journal:

1. Do you presently exercise regularly? Do you enjoy the type(s) of exercise you do?

2. When you examine your exercise practices and goals, where do you see the word "should" pop up the most?

Now start on a fresh page, and answer the following questions:

1. What, if any, is your idea of a "fun" way to engage in physical activity? This could be anything from walking to swimming to rock climbing.

2. Write a detailed description of how your mind and body would change if you integrated more aligned, fun forms of exercise into your schedule.

3. Mark at least one day per week on your calendar for exercise. If you don't exercise at all now, start small with 20 minutes, and work your way up.

You don't have to be perfect with exercise; you just have to get started. Once you start feeling the benefits, you won't want to stop. You'll become addicted to feeling healthy and energized.

Food

Food issues can be a heavy and deep-rooted topic, not to mention very sensitive for some people. Unfortunately, we have many external obstacles to deal with when it comes to eating healthily, such as wondering exactly what's in your food and where it's coming from. But, in addition, there may be internal obstacles to that you're trying to overcome, too, even if you may not be fully aware of them.

My biggest struggle with my current diet is:

The first and foremost thing to remember is not to put too much pressure on yourself. If you feel you need to make changes in your diet, choose something small to alter, and commit to it. Then, as you experience success with your first change, you can start to build on that, adding in another positive behavior as the last one becomes a steady habit. Maybe eliminating soda is the first step for you. Maybe next you'll choose to have one green juice per day, or two servings of leafy greens every day. Whatever it is, declare it, and stick to it.

A lot of people are extremists and think they have to do everything at once, making a complete 180-degree shift in their habits to see real change. While this might work for some people, the majority of us need to take things step by step. I strongly encourage you to avoid extremes, stay balanced, and make consistent progress by breaking goals down into smaller steps. Sound good?

When we're tripped up in old stories, it doesn't leave room for change to open up the new expanses in which serendipity occurs. Do you see how all of that mental junk takes up valuable space where big and exciting things could be happening? Yet when we finally clear all of that away, we send a signal to the universe that we are open to everything it has to offer us, and serendipity happens all of the time. Pretty cool, right?

9 LIVING WITH INTENTION

"An idea that is developed and put into action is more important than an idea that exists only as an idea."
                                                                    —BUDDHA

You've spent a lot of time and energy up to this point re-examining and rebuilding yourself to help bring more serendipity into your life. Everything you've been working on so far—from primary food to dejunking—is reshaping your current reality and energizing you into forward movement. Now it's time to get very specific on the direction in which you want that movement to happen.

The power to choose your own intention is one of the greatest you possess. Remember, every thought you have is a matter of choice. So it's time to cultivate the self-awareness you've created and turn toward living with purpose. If you don't articulate what you want, how can the universe and your loved ones support you? It also makes it really difficult for you to make choices and take action. It's like when you tune into a radio station, but you're just one number off—there's static. When you turn the dial to the exact station you want, the reception becomes clear.

What have you always wanted? If you don't declare it, it can't materialize. To get clarity on the steps you need to take, set a specific intention, and let the universe help you out. Tune in to the station that makes you feel your best—the one that makes you feel aligned with your dreams. Find out the non-negotiable things you need to do to feel tuned in to that station, and then do them consistently.

There's a big difference between the "what," "why," and "how" of the things you want to make happen. The "what" and "why" are all about dreaming big and getting really specific about what you want, and the "how" is all about allowing the universe to guide you in the next steps. Ask yourself what actions you will take and how you will want to feel and exist in the world.

This is an incredibly important time to get really honest with yourself, because if you don't, your intentions will be inauthentic and confusing to the universe. I want you to think about this: Are you honest with yourself in your life? Do you make excuses for yourself and other people? Are you speaking your truth from moment to moment? You're not helping anybody by being inauthentic, and it's exhausting.

When you're honest, you attract the people, things, and events that are right for you, and you keep the not-so-great stuff away. Therefore, you need to be totally honest when you set your intentions because the primary person you'll hurt by being dishonest is yourself. Try it today, and see how it goes. Be honest in every interaction, and notice when you're lying, even if it's about something small. This will take practice. So just begin by being aware of whether you're being authentic, and things will improve naturally.

PROFESSIONAL INTENTIONS

When I first started coaching, I would meet with clients in hotel lobbies because I couldn't afford office space. Everyone who worked at the hotels thought that I was a regular guest, and my clients really liked that environment. For me, I didn't care where I had to meet with them—my intention was simply to help people and to create a ripple effect to get as many people coaching as possible, so I just made it happen. I barely had any money at that time, but it was okay because I was fulfilling my intention of spreading my knowledge and helping other people live happy and healthy lives. Sometimes, you have to make sacrifices to live your mission and trust that you'll be guided.

Fast forward to 2005, a time when I was planning our new office space for Integrative Nutrition, located in the center of Manhattan. A feng shui master told me that the president of the school should have a prominent office with great energy. We decided it should be on the corner of the 12th floor, facing the street. Then, more recently, during one of my advisor's first months with the company, he was standing on the corner near our building and noticed an old advertisement on our façade that said "Rosenthal." And guess where it was? It was on the 12th floor, on the corner, right outside of the president's office. How cool is that? It's like the building was marked for my team and me—a sure sign of serendipity in action.

It was never my intention to live in a really nice house or have a lot of money; my intention was to support other people and teach them everything I knew so that they could move forward in their lives. I knew that everything else would fall into place if I stuck to my intention, even if that meant making some sacrifices in the moment. And everything did fall into place. Now I enjoy financial freedom, have an amazing life partner, and live in a beautiful home in the woods that supports my highly sensitive nature, allowing me to consistently recharge, reboot, and keep spreading my mission of health and happiness.

Serendipity is a big factor in one's career. When it comes to your mission and what you want to contribute to the world, it's important to follow the signs and stay in tune with universal rhythms. It's also key to ask yourself why you are doing the work that you do.

What is your personal career mission? What is your mission on a larger scale, for society or even the world? What impact do you want to have on others? How will it make you feel to create what you want to create? How much money do you want to make? Do you want to sit at an office, work from home, or work from coffee shops while you travel the world? Do you want to be indoors or outdoors? Work alone or with other people? When you set your intentions, it becomes obvious what you need to do to make things happen. Get clear on what you want, including as much detail as possible, and then watch your career align with your beliefs and personality as you begin to accomplish what you set out to create.

In addition, don't feel guilty about asking for help during this process. When students are starting out at Integrative Nutrition, I tell them to treat it like medical school, because it is. I recommend they email their family and friends and tell them that they are entering medical school and will be very busy during the year. I encourage them to outsource various tasks, like housekeeping and maybe childcare, so that they have time to focus on the work they truly want to do in the world. I want them to feel fully supported in fulfilling their mission and spreading the ripple effect.

What kinds of things in your life could you outsource so that you'll feel more supported and ensure you have the time to fully pursue living your ideal life? Part of setting intentions is helping yourself prioritize your tasks, allowing you to only spend your precious energy doing the things that inspire you. Maybe you could start using a laundry service, get an accountant and/or a virtual assistant, or start using a food delivery program? Once you've cleared your schedule of things you don't enjoy, you'll have more time to zero in on the specific actions you need to take to fulfill your intentions and focus your energy on high-leverage activities that you're good at.

SERENDIPITOUS MOMENTS

Professional Intentions

Tina

Five years ago, I quit my job and then got turned down for two jobs that I really wanted, which led me to two different part-time jobs and volunteer work, and then it led me to the perfect job a year later. This was a way better fit and experience than the two jobs that I thought I really wanted and got turned down for. I couldn't have been happier. That's how the universe works!

PERSONAL INTENTIONS

People are so worried about how they'll make things happen that they often don't even bother to dream about their ideal life. It's only once we code things as feasible in our brains that we can become truly limitless. I know it sounds cheesy, but if you can imagine it fully and say, "Yes, I can have this," then it's possible. The more centered you are in your body, mind, and heart, the more likely you are to be at one with everything around you. Just like the planets naturally align, we, too, naturally align when we're in balance and full of love. The secret to reaching that place of harmony and happiness? Love yourself first.

What intention for yourself physically would help you to love yourself? Maybe you want to feel light and energetic or strong and solid. How about emotionally? Popular emotional intentions are to feel whole, loved, calm, and inspired. These are just some ideas to get your imagination going—you don't have to choose any of these if you don't want to. Choose your words carefully. They should be a direct reflection of you.

Then, start thinking about the specific action steps you will need to take to get from where you are to where you want to be. Will you need to eat lots of vegetables, or maybe a good amount of protein? Experiment with food, exercise, and spirituality, and really tune in to how you're affected by your behavior in these areas.

In addition to setting intentions for yourself, you'll want to make sure your environment is set up in a way that's conducive to helping you reach your goals. Think about infusing your environment with the way you want to feel in your life. How can you create an environment where you can feel really good? Maybe you want to feel light in your body, and that means your environment needs to have good light, adequate healthy snacks, clean water, some plants, or all of the above. Every person is different. You might be noticing now that your home and/or work environments are not at all conducive to your intentions, and that's okay. Now that you know, you can take steps to change things. When you're in touch, you'll start to notice guideposts that lead you in the direction you're meant to go.

SERENDIPITOUS MOMENTS

Realizing Your Dreams

JoAnne

I had an idea of where I wanted to live, but didn't know where it was. And I knew I wanted to build a house, but wasn't sure how I would ever do it or be able to afford it. Then one day I decided to take the first step, so I visited a realtor to ask about properties for sale, even though I wasn't sure how it would work. I found a piece of land that I liked, and I decided that I could afford a loan payment. So I made the purchase. Suddenly, all of the other pieces started falling into place when a family member helped me connect with a contractor so that I could build my dream house. I have now been living in my fabulous home on my special piece of land for the last 7 years, and I'm still loving it!

Once you're feeling satisfied and empowered on your own, it's time to start thinking about relationships. After you fill up your own cup, so to speak, you can start really thinking about other people. That's not selfish; it's necessary. You need to give from a place of overflow, not lack, or else you're not really giving authentically.

The love you have for yourself is equal to the love you can accept from someone else. Before someone else can love you, you have to love yourself. And when you love yourself, serendipity starts appearing everywhere. You become a magnet for love and connection, and people can't help but be attracted to you. You might have to be very careful, because when you love yourself, you will attract so many people, and not all of them will be right for you. You'll have a lot of choices to make, and that's great. Choose wisely.

I know this woman who was studying to become an Integrative Nutrition Health Coach, and, when she got her practice up and running, she really started flourishing. She was doing work she loved and making a lot of money. Guess what happened next? She started attracting so many men that she had to turn down dates all of the time. Eventually, she met the man of her dreams, and they got married in Italy. It was such a cool thing to see and a great example of how all areas of primary food are connected.

Relationships are an important place to set clear intentions. How are you feeling in your relationships right now? Are you asking for what you need? Do you feel connected to like-minded people? What do you expect from your partner? How do you want to be treated? How will you treat your partner?

Before I met my life partner, I wasn't in a place where I felt like the energy I was putting into my relationships was being reciprocated. I'm naturally a giving person, and my work in the world is very generous. In meeting my partner, I finally found someone who is unconditionally giving and who supports me so much. She is also an incredible source of energy for me, giving me the fuel to keep doing my work in the world, and, amazingly, my work is also a way in which I can equally provide fuel to her. We have a beautiful give-and-take relationship, yet we're both independent. We don't complete each other, but, rather, we're two whole people coming together in an incredible way.

In relationships, a lot of people think you're supposed to spend every waking moment together, and that might work for some people. But, usually, it's counterproductive. My partner and I give each other a lot of space to reconnect with our selves, and that increases our serendipity. We know that we don't have to constantly be with each other to prove our affection, but we can come together when we choose. We also meditate together and dance together to stay in alignment.

All of these factors create a stable, loving situation in which both partners are in a place to attract a lot of serendipity. The bottom line is that when you're happy in your body, at ease in your mind, and fulfilled by your career, you will find the ideal partner and friends. Feeling really fulfilled in any one area of primary food directly affects the other areas. Fulfillment makes you produce more serotonin and other happy hormones, and then everything in your life starts to feel lighter and brighter. It's science, and it works.

Intentions are directly connected with serendipity. It might seem obvious that everyone would do well to figure out precisely what they want from life, but so many people just follow the steps that society prescribes, the steps they think they need to follow in the old paradigm: go to school, get a job, get married, and have kids. But the new paradigm is the only one you need to follow, one where you decide for yourself what you want, set intentions, and take small action steps every day. This approach does take clarity, honesty, and dedication, but once you start following it, everything you could possibly need and more will come easily to you. It's that simple.

CONCLUSION

"Learn how to see. Realize that everything is connected to everything else."

—LEONARDO DA VINCI

By now, you've acquired so many amazing tools to bring more serendipity into your life. We talked about gratitude and awareness, clearing out the clutter in your life, setting intentions, spirituality, community, connection, primary and secondary food, and more. So, how's it going? Do you feel that your daily life has entered into a more serendipitous era?

A DAY IN THE LIFE

Along with all of those tools to increase serendipity in your life, I also want to give you a snapshot into the life of a highly serendipitous person.

I'll use my friend, Lisa, an Integrative Nutrition Health Coach, as an example, and we'll look at one day in her life. Remember that there's no one-size-fits-all formula for living a serendipitous life. This is just one example that might spark your imagination and give you some ideas on how you want to structure—or not structure—your own days. Perhaps you thrive on a schedule, or maybe freedom and flexibility are the ingredients that fuel your creative process.

Here's a look into the typical day for Lisa:

7am — Wake up naturally with no alarm and meditate for 15 minutes

7:15am — Make green smoothie and tea

7:30am — Write morning pages and reflect on previous morning pages

8am — Light yoga and breathing exercises

8:30am — Get dressed and ready for the day

9:30am — Go for walk and admire nature; breathe in the beauty

10am — Start working with health coaching clients

5pm — End work and meditate

6pm — Join husband to relax and enjoy a glass of wine

7pm — Meet friends for dinner

9:30pm — Light stretches and breathing exercises; shut down media

10:00pm — Dry body brushing and hot bath or shower

10:30pm — Get into bed and calm the mind, slow the breathing, sleep

Which parts of this routine sound great to you?

Which parts do you dislike?

Which components, if any, do you see yourself integrating into your own life?

How might some daily rituals benefit your own life and increase your serendipity?

Write down your thoughts in your journal.

SERENDIPITOUS MOMENTS

Beautiful Synchronicity

Cynthia

Today has been filled with beautiful synchronicity. I glanced at my schedule for this week and thought to myself, "I could really use three more clients." Within 15 minutes, four people contacted me to become a client, and one more person an hour later.

Considering its effectiveness, I've now put in an order for an amazing husband, to be independently wealthy, and have the physique of a fitness model.

FINDING YOUR OWN SERENDIPITY

Look back in your synchronicity journal to the first week that you started reading this book, and then compare it with what you've written this week. Do you notice that you've started writing down more synchronistic and serendipitous events? Have you become more magnetic? Are you feeling happier and more in the flow? What are some changes you've noticed in your body, mind, career, and relationships? Let's take some time to reflect now.

Write down your 5 most memorable serendipitous events while reading this book.

1.

2.

3.

4.

5.

It's so important to learn from past events by acknowledging your progress, but it's also important to stay grounded and present by keeping track of synchronicity so that you can bring more of it into your life. One cool way to recognize that you're in a serendipitous flow is if you find yourself reading a book or watching a movie (did you know there's a movie called *Serendipity*?) or TV show that mirrors your own life and issues. Pay attention to these clues, and appreciate them. Now, ask yourself how you're going to keep moving forward? What are actions you'll take to stay in the flow? It's time to get excited about your future vision.

Write down the top 5 ways you're most excited to use what you've learned to keep moving forward.

1.

2.

3.

4.

5.

Serendipity plays such a huge role in your past, present, and the future. The tools I've laid out in this book have been so helpful to me in advancing my career and my personal life, and, as a result, I am happier now than I've ever been. I attribute so much of that success, both personally and professionally, to serendipity, something which I now experience daily. My one wish for you, as you finish this book and go out into the world with a refreshed outlook, is that you can share in all of the wonderful and positive changes I've experienced as a result of serendipity.

INDEX

SPREAD THE MESSAGE OF HEALTH AND HAPPINESS

Start a Career as an Integrative Nutrition Health Coach

The Institute for Integrative Nutrition is the world's largest nutrition school and a pioneer in the field of holistic health. With 100,000 students and graduates in 155 countries, we're transforming healthcare around the world!

Here's what students receive when they join IIN's cutting edge Health Coach Training Program:

STUDENT MATERIALS

VIBRANT COMMUNITY

LIVE EVENTS

NUTRITION EXPERTS

100,000 STUDENTS AND GRADUATES IN 155 COUNTRIES

CERTIFICATIONS

Integrative Nutrition's advanced courses are taking Health Coaches to the next level with in-depth training:

- Advanced Business Course
- Launch Your Dream Book
- Coaching Mastery Course
- Hormone Health Course
- Gut Health Course
- Emotional Eating Psychology
- International Health Coach University

VISIT OUR WEBSITE TO GRAB OUR CURRICULUM GUIDE OR SIGN UP FOR A **FREE SAMPLE CLASS!**

www.integrativenutrition.com